PERSONAE

Personae

and other selected poems

PETER ABBS

SKOOB BOOKS PUBLISHING
LONDON

First versions of sections from this collection were originally
published in Great Britain as follows:

For Man and Islands   Tern Press June 1978
Songs for a New Taliesin   Tern Press (Limited Edition) 1981
                    Gryphon Press (Trade Edition) 1981
Icons of Time   Gryphon Press 1991

Published in 1995 by
SKOOB BOOKS PUBLISHING LTD
11a-17 Sicilian Avenue
Southampton Row
Holborn
London WC1A 2QH

First edition

Series editor: Christopher Johnson
Design © Mark Lovell

Pottery by Martin Spanyol

ISBN 1 871438 77 2

Printed by Ling Wah Press Sdn. Bhd.

Acknowledgements

Some of the poems in this volume have been previously published in: *Acumen, Anglo-Welsh Review, Arvon Foundation Poetry Anthologies 1980* and *1987, Blue Nose Poetry Anthology 1993, Country Life, Critical Enquiry, Critical Quarterly, Forward Book of Poetry 1993, Human World, Illuminations, The Independent, The Observer, Outposts, Poetry Wales, Spokes, Stand, Tar River Poetry (USA), Use of English, Western Mail, Y Saeth* and in the volumes *For Man and Islands* (1978), *Songs of a New Taliesin* (1981) and *Icons of Time* (1991).

By the same Author

We make our necessities by our choice of gods

Virgil

Poetry is the plough that turns up time

Osip Mandelstam

Contents

Personae

Preface

I believe the function of poetry is essentially mythic and healing. It is my hope, then, that the poems gathered here give expression to this deep impulse for symbolic ordering and reparation. Certainly the poems are attempts - how successful only the reader can judge - to place the truths of the heart in the house of imagination. I also hope they are accessible to any one who would care to understand them. For if poetry is to survive it is now imperative that we close the gap between poetry and society.

The collection *Personae* is published here for the first time; the other poems have been taken from earlier collections: *For Man and Islands* (1978), *Songs of a New Taliesin* (1981) and *Icons of Time* (1991). In the case of the first two volumes I have selected a number of representative poems and also altered their sequence; but, as it is finally conceived as a single long poem, *Icons of Time* is reprinted in its entirety. I have resisted the temptation to revise. Apart from altering some punctuation and deleting an occasional word, the poems in this edition remain true to their original formulation. They may also allow the reader to discern a certain progression from the poems written in the 70s to the poems written in the 90s.

Quite what that progression is, it is almost impossible for me to say. What I do see, quite clearly - and for the first time - is a recurring movement from autobiography to myth, from the concern with place and identity in *From Man and Islands* to a preoccupation with persona and myth in *Songs of a New Taliesin*, to be repeated a second time in the subsequent movement from *Icons of Time* to *Personae*. There is a distinct pattern here, a movement from the heart to the imagination back to the heart and so on. I do not clearly understand it but I sense its rhythm and power and can only hope that the sequence may release a similar movement in my reader and, in so doing, bring poetry closer to our common lives again.

Peter Abbs
Summer 1993

from

For Man And Islands

1978

PRELUDE

Where would you lead
  me and what
      would you have of
me, restless
  and enigmatic
      spirit? In
the enclosed garden
  it is again
      Autumn. Sycamore
leaves litter the
  small paths -
      the jagged leaves'
edges are turned
  inwards and everywhere
      their yellowness is
marred and blotched
  with blight. In
      the garden
the lemon light grows
  faint. Yet what
      are *you* doing
here, lover of
  strange mists and burning
      aromas,
at the open
  gate standing with
      the palms of your
hands showing? Will
  you wait as
      I approach and
let me read and
  go where the lines
      take me?

THE WORD

You suggest and
provoke until
I chase,

chase you wherever
you will
I would, but

where do you
go,
down which

turning, into
which
unused chapel of truth,

so many the turnings,
crosses,
ends, I do not know,

yet, tantalizer, how
can I
forget how

you beckon so, what
you would
promise

in your lithe movement,
not to be mine,
grace

in my city,
out
of my power.

A GIFT

Eithin ni bu fad Taliesin. The Gorse was never prized.

Dawn smokes. I see
Gorse crackle over the slate's
Face. It swarms like bees. Is more
Imperious than
Torc or blazoned disc
Burnished. An emblem of transcendence. Each
Flower has
Power to heal the gashed memory -
And put out to sea
The prudent heart.

Ishtar -
Astarte -
Aphrodite -
Magdalene -

I bring to you what things I can,
Things despised,
Unprized, spiked, feral.
This morning I bring
From the rock's throat, cynghanedd
Of barbed beauty.

Strange goddesses, do not turn your calm heads,
Nor let me disturb your coma.
I would not have your
Immortal litanies
Overheard
And put on record.

Now silence alone protects us.

WHO WAS IT?

Who was it, yesterday, at the window
Of my dark room,
With a young girl's lips
Incanting a language sweeter than honey:
Arms yellow as laburnum flowers
With long delicate fingers
Lifted and, for one moment, beckoning?

And why did I, in an age worn through
With too much doing, not follow?
Why did I turn back
To my desk, to shuffle again
This pale pack of abstractions,
Familiar and dead,
With only myself to deal to?

And what, as I turned over
First archaic Queen, then King,
Was that sudden sensation
As of a cloud passing?
A shiver of breath.
A stillness. And on my forehead
The clammy touch of death.

INTO THE DARK

From time into
time,
into time, no
thing
survives.

Tonight as we touch
our hands are cold.

Wind levels. And
levels. And to whatever monuments
the clock tocks
pyramids in time are sand, sand desert.

Our limbs weigh
with the weight of centuries.

While love's elusive child rushes
into the dark,
scattering
his bold red fire.
Into
the dark.

We die
as we whisper.

And what things remain
mould,
go slowly
to this desert of slow
wind lulling forever
desert.
Desert.

Tonight our bed is passion's coffin.
Cold.

Dust settles.
Love. Universe. Poem.
Still.

And old.

IT

It skulks in the mind's undergrowth
In the dark thickets
It quivers close to the bed of rivers
A snake through the conflagration of grass
It is acquainted with stones and roots
Has wound itself many times round
The dripping tentacles of nature

At dusk it flies through the warp and weft of shadows
Compounds the darkness
Till large familiar things loom forward
Bulked with strangeness
Blackness humped upon blackness
Through which it lilts and slips

Where do I stand but where it was
And is no longer though
Something of its essence always lingers
Hangs frailly in the morning
From the bent bough's sodden foliage
Pervades a corner of the garden
A turning of the road

Disquieted I poke the ground
Dank arching grass blank stones
A thistlehead unloads its seeds
A bird flits through the charcoal thickets
The silence drums
I tread near the edge of some archaic memory
I can never reach
And spill a brief life writing
To allay the ache of it

WINTER SOLSTICE

And so we enter the dark hours of the winter solstice.
Lime green lichen seeps down the damp walls of this house.
The day sags like a farmer's sack hung out to dry.
Clouds, trees, grass, stare back, blank and immobile.
Even the sea presses on its dark bed of bladderwrack and weed,
Lifeless as a hunk of quarried stone.
And the small life of this cramped village continues as usual.

I listen to the wind. Its long blades cut
Through the corrugated sheds and shacks that wound these fields.
It brings to this chimney insubstantial lamentations,
Sounds that flock and beat their charred wings
Like memories stolen out of caves and catacombs,
Too dark and distant to possess a name -
Yet scrape the bone beneath the skin.

I will not listen to them, the wind's wailing, the dark voices,
The frozen underside of the burning sun.
We switch on the news again and watch
The tail-end of a civilisation slide and twitch
In the dust, determined neither to retreat nor run.
I look outside. Starless and drizzling the night hangs.
I confront my absurd quest. Nothing achieved. Nothing done.

AS DESCARTES

I wake late.
The window's half-opaque
With streaming rain.
The barn's washed

Out. A cow's giant back
Smudges the grass black,
Flecks the wet world -
Canvas. A gust

Hurls a bird-shape
Over the wall where mountainous
Clouds collide and slide
East south east. Nothing's pegged in -

All's slack and flapping.
At the top of the slang
Wind teases the tree's
Foliage, the sycamore's matt -

Backed leaves hang strangely
Outwards. The stream's too turbid
To return the day.
It rolls its own stones,

Froths over boulders.
A poet should be out
In this, his mind coinciding
With all that flows and

Undergoes metamorphosis,
Minister to the conjugating
Universe, not thinker.
Yet I will go to my desk again,

Perverse as Descartes. I will hold
Up the strands that tie me in
And with the blades of my questioning
Cut the world-web, always

Seeking stasis.
I will censor the influx
Of my senses,
The coarse gang of voices
Which squall outside my window
Calling. I will empty this hot
And crowded place and wait.
And wait.

Imageless, still
Before the blank paper.
Growing
Anxious.

THE DEATH OF THREE COCKS

He came punctually, at eleven, the hour he said.
I took him to the shed.
He upturned the first bird
And slipped the knife into its neck -

More crimson than its crown
The blood dripped to the ground -
Shocking in its redness -
And with one hand he kept the rent

Neck down. Mildly, he said
I have seen this since I was a child
Following the heels of the butcher
Round the farms.

With a kind of inward dread I took
The dead bird from his hands.
There was such commotion in its legs
And pinions, it appalled to hold it.

Obedient to the last transmission
Of the will, its mottled wings
Still fluttered, shut and shuddered.
Would not stay still.

Yet I must stand and watch
The next two go, wedged upside down between
The farmer's legs, to know
That somewhere in that ruffled sheen

My neighbour's knife had broken through
And watch the bird's panic and premonition ebb
As across their bright bead eyes
Slowly the coarse lids drooped and set.

Furtively, I shovelled soil upon the blood.
The children must not know nor guess.
It is the last time! Once is enough! I said.
For hours I gathered up the incriminating fluff.

At the farm that afternoon another batch of cocks were bled.

THE SACK OF LEARNING

1

Outside Rome, tonight, the barbarian
Camp-fires are bright, ablaze
With ancient manuscripts.
Above the scattered tents,
Scorched with a new image
Of Faith become savage,

The red flags swirl
And whip the stars.
Inside the city walls,
Sent by indignant powers,
Thirty thousand troops rape,
Murder, burn and mutilate.

It has happened all
Before: the rueful acts,
Inclement crimes. Turbulence
Joining turbulence to call
Out the asylum of the mind,
Untether the straddling animal.

But all is well:
For pious men with shaven heads,
Stabling their horses in looted shrines,
Know their Divinity is free
To upend *idolatrous times*;
Annihilate ornate history.

2

A prisoner in Castel Sant Angelo,
Pope Clement strolls,
Long hair and beard,
Against the darkness quoting Job.

3
In one brief night
By Lutheran and lout

The giant tap-root of the mind
Pulled out

The tree's fabulous foliage
Set alight.

4
On the brow of the hill
Where clouds raise
And erase
Themselves and streams begin,
Watching, stand this King and Queen:
Immortal and primordial.
They seem
To gaze upon the distant edge of things,
The morning's mist that might be mellow
With the sun's splay of light -
Now blotched with smoke,

As from all sides, flames
And further flames encroach.

BRECHFA

Bearing torn leaves, wrenched twigs,
From the shorn wood
The wind has come against our home.
Down these black cavernous chimneys
It has jabbed its harsh fingers
Wanting what was once its own;
And through every crack and rusted keyhole
Thrust its long knife blades.
And shuddered in the window-sills.

And, foolishly, we had undone the small
Improvised defences of wiser generations;
Wrenched from holes and hidden ledges
The cobwebbed rags and matted wool
And pulled from the door's edges
The thin hardboard slats
Nailed far into the rotting wood
And in the garden burnt them.

And yet, again, this long Welsh house
Has held its ground.
Its slated roof, its mud-bound walls,
Its quarry tiles still stand, sound
And unbroken. Like Nature's shell, it shelters
Whatever scrap of life should enter
Seeking its own rhythm and pattern.

And now its doors and windows open
To a gentler morning.
In the garden, bracken fronds unfurl
Their cool heraldic beauty.
On old land between old walls,
My tongue feels free to move and praise
A rush of moments which,
Beyond all reason,
Now swell and shake like buds
Shadowing the house in this green season.

EVENING AFTER THE MAELSTROM

for the Darlington Family

It is evening, after the maelstrom,
After the upturning,
Burning and devastation of cities,
As reported on radio
And (briefly) on television.
And prophesied in the last newspapers.

The herd stand by the farm's gate,
Dumb and enduring;
Even in this breeze, bitter
With mountain mist and drizzle,
Their ribbed flanks are calm as boulders,
Only their frayed tails twitching.

They have stood there
Ten thousand years, bulging
Eyes staring down
The dark track, trailing back
Through the charred centuries
To the first spark of history.

Slathering, their warm breath
Wreathes the air; they await
Man's archaic canticle to cattle,
And a half-simple girl who wades
Slowly through the slang's
Slop and mud to guide them in.

The door opens on to dusty hay,
Bedding for a dozen animals.
Through the dark slates' cracks light
Needles the barbarian night.
Inside, at the finger's touch,
Thick milk drums into the pails.

FOR MAN AND ISLANDS

Today I walk the winter's beach, blind
To the flecked waves
Rising to the wind's pull,
Blind to beauty -
For the time's intolerant images
Storm my mind.

I find not waves but faces
Marching to the Age:
Faces numb with the cold wash of phrases,
Faces frozen with slogans,
Eyes swollen to flashing discs,
Minds hardened by helmets.

Between the waves the crowds surge
Hedgehogged with hurtling glass.
Dark blood tars the shore.
I see a child without limbs,
His arms blown to spray.
One bent hand floats like a claw.

I look out to sea and pray
For man and islands. I think of
Skellig Michael. Iona. Lindisfarne.
I see their jagged foreheads
Gazing back, their clenched fists
Raised above the water -

And I pray that their black-cracked rocks
Be ready to hold the storm-borne
Seeds again, to shield whatever
Fragile spores of hope may -
Though our times seem sterile - fall,
Be there to cradle what is new, once more.

from

Songs Of A New Taliesin

1981

THE TREE OF KNOWLEDGE

And the Lord God said, 'Behold the man is become as one of us,
to know Good and Evil'.

Genesis Ch. 3 v. 22.

And in the cool of the evening
God
     slept
satisfied. And in the tree's
  shadow
     Adam
drew close to Eve and knew
  her for
     the first
time. And in the darkness of
  touching her
     his tongue,
adept as ever,
  rhapsodic,
     named her,
proclaimed her. And Eve took
  with awe
     love's
sticky stem till its nodding bud
  burst into
     flower, burst into
seed, deep, deep inside her. A high
  tide, their
     sighing
filled the whole garden. And
  subsided. Then
     one body
drawing the same breath, they dreamt
  the first
     dream
as they slept. The serpent uncoiled,
  rehearsed
     the next scene.

II

In the morning Eve woke
   to take
      the serpent's
apple. And walking through
   the garden
      she moved
         elated, loving more and more the taste
of her single
      self, self -
created. Querulous, she returned
   to Adam:
      In love
who is who? I'm not myself
   when I'm in you
      and who are you
when you're in me?
   Love's condition
      is not
free. Adam took the fruit
   and both advanced
      to suffer
love's dilemmas. Alone, they desired
   to be together;
      together
they conspired to be apart; they met
   to squabble;
      parted
to idealise. Painfully they unlearnt
   each other,
      no longer
sure if hate might lie beneath
   the smile
      or love
behind the grimace. Could not
   accept nor
      yet
escape what both half -
   ached for,

                    half -
repudiated. The apple-bite became
        the love-bite.
                    That night
restless, apart, they dreamt the second
        dream. The serpent
                    left
the fading tree, slid into the dark,
        the garden closed -
                    imperceptibly.

                    III

God woke apalled, mind somehow
        dismembered,
                    body,
somewhere bleeding, hauled into
        a future
                    He had not
foreseen, could not recognise.
        Divided, the lovers
                    crawled
out from His dream, held
        firm His
                    flailing arms.
Locked together, lurching
        forwards and backwards
                    and sideways,
they left dark stains on trees,
        on rocks;
                    at every cross
and turning left crimson tracks.
        At the small
                    gate
into history, a limping god slumped
        upon two mortal
                    backs.

GOOD FRIDAY

And on the Friday
Mary Magdalene
Came to her Christ

Hung on the cross
A noble bird
Stripped of his plumage

His white skin ripped
His quivering wings
Pinned to the wood

And she lay with him
And in his great pain
He made manifest his love

And on the next day
The bloody tree
Burst into bud

And migrating flocks perched
On his outstretched arms
And there was song.

THIS NOMADIC GOD

1

When the god was born on the hill we stayed inside.

2

When we spotted in the valley his bloody caul making the stream all red,
Somewhat repelled we walked away.

3

When on the same night we stared into his great eye
Glaring through our window we switched off the light;
We said *There can be no such thing.*
Not in our times, 2,000 Anno Domini.

4

When in the darkness he dared to rise through the basement of our house
We fumbled for the light and cried *Ah! Dreams! - and their archaic*
remnants.
For we had read the literature. And sighed, relieved.

5

Later, when the trees' leaves shrivelled yellow -
Later, when the bent bracken bled profusely -
Later, when the low snow clouds shed their icy shingle -
Later, when the white river no longer flowed but lay nailed to its own
bed -
If you remember we were both rather busy;
There were forms to sign, bills to clear,
And the house - it stood in constant need of attention and repair.

6

Yet still the conjuror-god casts his signs about,
Daily scrawls his icons on the shifting sands,
Above reeling cities brushes his gentle ideograms,
On concrete slabs executes his reckless graffiti.

7

And still, on random days, he knocks on our locked door
Many times. Incisive knocks. Insistent. What would he have of us?
This trickster salesman, this nomadic god? If we let him in,
Would he annihilate our private space?
At our table does he want a simple place?
Is it that he wants a glass of wine? A slice of bread?
Two stale lives to transubstantiate?

THE SINGING HEAD OF ORPHEUS

Dismembered, his limbs sunk quickly but much
As we pressed down his severed head it rose
In its own blood, exultant. Words streamed through
His gaping mouth. Half-seeing our deed for
What it was, we screamed, became hysterical -
Till caught in the river's tidal run
The singing head moved on beyond our reach;
In the main current it tossed and spun
A floating gargoyle, throat open to the sun.
Late that evening we could still hear
Out beyond the estuary, his canticum,
Head lifted in a silver track of light.
In its wake there flew a mob of gulls,
Their sleek black-headed skulls tilted low to
The water. Some said they were charmed by
His power of song. But we Mænads knew why
The birds shrieked, what it was they waited for.
When it became too dark to see, when we
Could no longer hear the song - or had
It ended? We each returned to separate
Beds. I slept badly. In a dream Orpheus
Came to me and said: *I sing because
When I stop the world will end.* Then I felt
About me a chaos of wings and claws -
The unadorned war of descending beaks.
I saw the god's bright face slit to pieces.
I woke and shivered at the deed I'd done.
I shivered for all men born of flesh
And trembled at the holocaust to come.

THE RETURN OF THESEUS TO ARIADNE

Tradition falsifies. I did not slay the minotaur.
It is true holding Ariadne's twine I descended
The black and airless labyrinth and, true,
That at a great depth I found the creature
Steaming in its own filth. Its two eyes
Like slits cut in the black back of matter
Examined me. I shouted *Minotaur*! and, at once,
We engaged in a heroic battle, in the pose
The story tellers clamour for. Yet that embrace
Was my undoing. Holding him in my hands
I lost the appetite to kill. He became
A murky mirror in which I glimpsed myself:
His slit eyes, I knew, were mine, blind
In the darkness of my own mind; his limbs
Urged me to sense the contours of my own body,
Amoral source of things. Even his grunts
Stirred memories down so deep I could not
Fathom them. So I lost the will to slay him
And in the end breathless, after much blood, we made
Our pact: I would daily descend to feed him
And, in return, though loath, he agreed to learn
My symbols. Dazed, I return slowly, holding
The twine, the single strand, faithful to the end.
And at the cave's entrance Ariadne held me
Caressed my torn flesh, kissed my sores;
She did not avert her eyes but with such love
Received all I had brought from the minotaur -
Who, as we lay, far below us settled.

TALIESIN THROUGH THE SEASONS

Wyv cerdoliad; wyv saer mal dryw
I am a musician - an artificer like the wren.

Inside the cycle
I dance and I dance.
I am Taliesin.
Master of trance.
Moulder of patterns.
Remembrancer.
An artificer like the wren.

It is winter. It is dawn.
Upon the frozen dead
A flint rain falls.
The river's turbulent flow
And undulation's over -
Flat as a gravestone
Slab it lies; all that was
Living, stiff and brittle,
Gripped within it.

I am Taliesin
I dance a slow dance.

Comes the spring, ice snaps
And cracks, the river
Groans - through gaps
The long locked water
Seeps up like poetry.
In a bright light
Cobwebbed with shadows,
World traffics in ice-floes.

I am Taliesin.
I dance and I dance.

It is summer and noon.
Under the burning stone
Blanched roots splay
Out, restless as antennae,
Restless as life;
Eyeless, through warm
Earth, the worm
Winds to the light.

I am Taliesin.
I dance and I dance.

Autumn comes, comes the dusk.
Christ hangs from
Every tree - His side split
Like a bursting husk.
His drops of blood
Are the leaves
Pouring down.
They sear the ground.

I am Taliesin.
I dance a sad dance.

Inside the cycle
I dance and I dance.
I am Taliesin.
Master of trance.
Moulder of patterns.
Remembrancer.
An artificer like the wren.

WELSH NATIVITIES

It is bitter cold. Each blade of grass
Bent down by frost. Tremulous pools in the churned
Slang's ruts are frozen still. New on this New
Year's Day the sun stares and winks from the crest
Of the hill. Bright as percussion, as
Burnished brass, in a hundred frames, the glass
Throws back its light, returns a darker burning,
A greater conflagration. On every roof
The plum-fleshed slates begin to weep. And through
The streets come children running to an old
Ceremony, move from door to door knocking
And singing *Calennig* and *Blwyddyn Newydd*
Dda. Each child clutching in his red raw
Fist whatever pence are thrown at him
And even in this whipping wind the village
Doors are open to let in the dying
Language on the children's lips - as always
On the furthest edge, on the periphery
Of Empire. And in the quiet theatre of
My room I ask one thing: that here under
This harsh lamp's light, my mind's womb may push out
New births, Christ-child-poems, new thoughts, new feelings,
New imaginings, fleshed most beautifully
With hearts beating and on their lips breath's red
Roses. At the edge, on the world's periphery.

from

Icons of Time

An Experiment in Autobiography

1991

I

Prologue

I have searched for myself

Heraclitus

A COSMIC STORY

And now, feeling querulous, God said *Let*
There be consciousness. And slept. And out
Of his long dream confused man stepped.
Scorched victim of divine fission.
Crazed animal dipped into time.
And under the mushrooming cloud and through
The black snow crept towards the crime
Of his history, immolating his own kind -
For there was this burn and ache in his side
Which nothing, for long, could assuage or cool,
Nor could he recognise the darker face,
Reflected back from the cracked world's pool.
And God woke from his dream. And half-understood.
Sensed the nails through the palms. And the chafing wood.

RETURNING TO SHERINGHAM

I walk the promenade. Half-familiar faces
Drift past me, so much less monumental
Than I remember, so badly cracked. And faded.
In their canvas tents the same women
Sit. Still. Knitting. Staring out.
A brackish wind blisters the day. I go
Up the steps to our old house - how it
Has shrunk! Under the salt-laden breeze paint
Has peeled. Black cracks in the wood are deeper.
Hedge and gate have been wrenched out to make
A parking space. Now only a summer-house -
Vacant half the year. How did we ever
Live here cocooned in such a claustrophobic place?
Across geometric lawns unknown children shout.

WAITING FOR THE HARVESTER

Here I stood in the crew-cut stubble,
Sharp stone in hand waiting for the harvester
To turn upon the final strip of wheat,
To see the hares dart wide-eyed into the gun's
Explosion or rise like crimson rags upon
The blades. Now, near the same spot, I can
Hardly recognise the self I was;
Now I am no longer armed - I move
Across the earth, mesmerised; myself
Trapped in the last small track of wilderness.
At every footfall, at every dog bark,
Every quiver of the vast machine, I shudder.
Sense in my flesh my own sharp stone;
The damp blades whirring above dry bone.

A FURTHER VISIT: FEBRUARY 1990

for my Mother

Back - and at each glance the town contracts.
How dwarf the buildings seem that once towered
Over me. All close-ups then; and sticky palms.
We take the bitter route along the promenade.
You talk of the latest deaths, lives slowly
Extinguished, last words said. At each return
There are further casualties to add. The sea
Is out; the iron defences bleed an oxide red.
At the cemetery we clear the grave. You plant
A rose. I touch the stone, sense Father's back:
White. Emaciated. Cold. A frenzied wind
Tears at our throats. The driven clouds blacken
The sun. I kiss you from the moving train.
The scene blurs behind me. It begins to rain.

ABSENCE

I have been here before, chest pressed
Against the stone's worn ledge, feeling the same
Unease as I do now, peering through the gloom
And silence to the abrupt stop of water.
Through the darkening clouds, criss-cross of boughs,
My face stares back. Mouth bearded, wrinkled brows.
An actor's mask whose parts I do not recognise,
Whose lines I can no longer read. Hamlet
Without an audience? More like Narcissus -
Only myself here, under alternating focus.
What did I, a child, throw down this well?
A gap exists where the syntax ends.
There's a numbing sense of loss. Nothing
Comes back. This silence where these shadows toss.

WHO I AM

He did not observe that with all his efforts he made no advance - meeting no resistance that might, as it were, serve as a support upon which he could take a stand, to which he could apply his powers, and so set his understanding in motion.

Kant

What is it that I do? This dizzy spinning
Of myself. This geometric cobweb that I make
From my own entrails. Intractable substance,
Obsessively shaped to a fine thread.
Part fact. Part fabulation. An obscure agent
In me fashioning the dark strands into pattern.
A design, somehow redemptive, however difficult.
What was could not have been otherwise.
There's a kind of freedom in admitting it.
Facts are weights. They tether random flight,
The delusions of Icarus, the Romantic type.
Filament by filament, inch by inch, I make
This architecture: a bound and limited life.
What I have struggled with is who I am.

II

Fragments From A Catholic Childhood

'I rhyme
To see myself to set the darkness echoing'

Seamus Heaney

PREMATURE BIRTH

Surname: Abbs. *First names*: Peter Francis.
Date of birth: 22.2.42. *Place*: Cromer.
The facts console. Deceive and mesmerise.
Yet mother's story has a nightmare ring.
All the way to the theatre she had screamed:
I want to die, I want to die, I want -
Until the gas took over. Born premature -
Cut from the womb three months too soon -
I choked into the commotion of hands, the glare
Of swivelling lights, muffled blare of plenitude.
Mother sighed *A girl? A girl?* and bitter, wept.
For her: scars from the surgeon's knife.
For me: slow, impeded waking into life.

AT THE OAK WOODS

This morning, not as it usually is.
Not box-hedge, nor black currant, nor mint's aroma.
Merely the breeze tapping the window pane -
And Grandmother's there. With pins, with clips, she plaits
Her hair. Grandfather's sipping tea from his saucer.
I've slipped the intervening years again.
On the fire branches froth, sizzle, blaze, smoulder.
The varnished chairs shimmer like manufactured glass,
Their curving legs are tongues of fire.
I go down the green passage to the open door,
Splinters of God lie in the melting grass.
The marigolds stand erect; orange and oracular.
I go through the walled garden to the pond.
A goldfish surfaces. Circles. And is gone.

IN THE WOODSHED

In the corner of the garden was the shed.
Across the door a fig tree arched, and spread.
Warmed by the sun its ribbed fruit hung down;
A ripe purple stained the outer rind.
Yet the palmate leaves were hands prohibitive;
They joined to shut one out. When pushed,
The door swung open. Inside it was illicit
Dark. Chill underground. I paused - time passed -
Then tiptoed down. Slowly **they** materialised:
In a corner kindling limbs were stacked and bound.
Serrated teeth gleamed from each black side.
A hacked torso rose up from the ground.

A nightmare rides rough-shod upon my sleep.
I was in too far. And down too deep.

UNREAD SIGNS

Earth was littered with signs we did not read
Nor comprehend. In gaping pits we picked
Glossy blackberries or collected from the ground
Cold metal shapes, long, tapered, with frilled edges
Chock-full with grit and sand. Harder than shale
Whatever force had forged them, they were made to last.
Blankly we accepted them, bits from dislodged turf,
Fragments of the sliding screes we tried to scale.
Barbed wire poked through bramble thickets
Or dangled, flaking, from the cliff's ledges.
We dived into a labyrinth of tunnels
Rank with urine and discarded papers:
Shells exploded, ships sank, burning cities fell -
We hurtled through the black, blind, ephemeral.

THE LOOK-OUT TOWER IN
THE OAK WOODS

We saw only what our guileless games allowed;
Assumed the shelter's womb led out towards
The light. Always summer. The sea a sheet
Of wrinkled blue (on blue) with puffs of cloud;
No shadows ran along the silent beach -
Norfolk's backdrop to our blindfold play.
In the Oak Woods we climbed the look-out tower.
We leapt the missing steps. From the broken top
We watched the yellow squares streaked with scarlet
End abruptly with the shore. Low tide.
Stranded on the white chalk bed, a mine
Stared back at us with one blank eye.
But we stood up high, salt on our lips and brow,
Safe on the rotting planks - the moment, always now.

MYRTLE COTTAGE AT WEST RUNTON

The West Runton Abbs were Methodists.
They ate meat on Fridays, placed no crucifixes
On the mantelpiece, read *Pilgrim's
Progress* and *The Methodist Recorder. Papists!*
Grandmother spits out the word like it burns
Her mouth. Grandfather keeps himself apart.
Where the coast road turns to Roman Camp
He sits on the village bench. And talks Socialism.
*I don't believe in any God you dress
Up for,* he says. *And read between the lines!*
All his life he laboured for the genteel classes
He most despised. In Myrtle Cottage
A wood fire glows. Dark above the old bureau
An antlered stag stands high, where water flows.

THE OTHER CHILD

I look through the window of my first school:
St Josephs. R.C. Sheringham. Norfolk.
Through the pane of fractured glass I stare
Into that silent chamber, sunk from mind.
Silver radiators still stand by the dark green
But all the trappings - abacus, globe,
Charts, blackboard, maps - have long since gone.
Was I ever here? Learning God by rote?
Obscure eel in the shallow tank of learning -
Even then forgetful of names, dates, facts.
I cannot find the child I was. Nothing
Coheres. Or coincides. Or rhymes.
The school door's locked; the place is out of bounds.
A pensive boy inside does not turn round.

ST PETER'S COLLEGE FOR
CATHOLIC VOCATIONS: 1954

I mourn the child I seldom was. Precarious
At birth. Washed up, at last. At St Peter's
College. Freshfields. Liverpool. A pale
Face elongated with piety. Alabaster
Hands clutching the plastic beads. Or clasped
Before the fourteen Stations of the Cross.
Baroque actor straining to shed the child
Who seldom was. Who cried himself to sleep
While the Mill-Hill Fathers' red sashed cassocks
Cracked and slapped against our wooden cells.
And priests in black gowns were walking their rounds
And binding with briars my joys and desires.

Dear child, I would tell you if I could...

A stricken deer makes for the shadowed wood.

THE ECZEMA OF CHRIST

I remember your raw hands, first. And now
I see your face. Scored red. And white with flaking.
The eczema of Christ! And your name? What was your name?
Was it Bailey? Slowly you said something
Like: *Go to the Loaches...It's the best place.*
It stank of excrement. But you were right.
The blocked homesickness streamed down my face.
That night I watched the Liverpool-Southport
Trains glide by. Each lonely passenger glowed
With a freedom I conferred upon them.
Mundane life - that lost beatitude!
On Friday nights we confess on bended knees.
We scour our soiled imagination clean.
A sick Christ dangles from the plastic beads.

AN UNDELIVERED LETTER

Oh, but Christ, you were hooked on prayer.
Your cocaine rosary, your litany of valium,
Your cheap narcotics always at hand,
Available whenever the going got rough -
Or our exams came. Hunched in the church,
Small hands barricading your face, lips
Pursed up against the world's violation.
All that sacrifice! All those prayers! -
As the day-trippers mobbed past outside.
We felt we could not turn Cliff Road
Without the intercession of the saints.
And I, ham actor, sick to please
Tried to outstrip the illustrious saints for years,
Addicted to the dark, violet, heart-shaped words.

THE DEATH OF GRANDMOTHER 1960

I was eighteen when Grandmother died.
She had fainted at the Catholic fete.
Was deep in a coma when we reached her side.
She recognised none of us.

Our agitated words sink into silence.
Your face hangs a crumpled mask come loose;
Somewhere your life edges into blackness;
The beads I give you dangle like a noose.

And she who filled our lives with so much talk
Died alone without a single word.
I look at you now in your wedding photograph;
Demure. More beautiful that I remember.

Any second your mouth will burst into a smile.
Your animal eyes hungry for their future.

IN THE MUSEUM

Unceremoniously they lay that ancient
Body out, unwrap the limbs. One by one,
Peel back the binding resin rinds.
With scalpels cut the pad of chaff and mud.
They number every bone. Brush, weigh and pack
The crumbling aromatic dust; unstring
The pious tags and take the last frail sheaves
Of faith, centuries of hope, dissolving.
Yet what do these masked surgeons work
To find under the scents and gnostic tricks
Of Anubis? Naked on the block
A human mortal lies: H7386;

Her hollow head, tilted back, rapacious
Mouth open, still gagging on the nothingness.

THE LOSS OF FAITH

What did we do when we unchained the earth from its sun?
...Are we not plunging continually?
...Are we not straying as through an infinite nothing?
                                                    Nietzsche

Who put the neon-lighting of his childhood
Out? A juke box throbs with *Jail House Rock*.
He reads Karl Marx and dreams of freedom.
He smooths his hair with daubs of Brylcreem.
Gone from the Eucharist, where is God?
On Sheringham sands *I can connect nothing*
With nothing. The spray lashes into the dark.
In my own town I have become a stranger.
I kneel and pray before the blessed virgin -
My mind's a stew where Magdalene strips.
I enquire of all that lives its final aim.
The ornate dome of faith cracks and splits.
God created the world *ex nihilo*. And withdrew.
Then, one day, the nothingness seeped through.

III

Father and Son

Spirit gains its truth only by finding itself in absolute dismemberment

Hegel

TONGUE-TIED

Father, now when I speak, I speak for you.
The silence you maintained could not be kept.
A knife, it spliced our mutual lives in two.
Tongue-tied, we were forever awkward. And inept.
Silence was our dumb inheritance.
The suicidal note passed down to us:
Keep your tongue still. Keep your mouth shut -
Numbing contract of our rural class.
The laconic words were slowly drawled
To damn our thoughts and keep the feelings dark.
Nothing. Say nothing. Say nothing at all.
The anger mounting in the throat was swallowed back;
And swallowed back it became all hell to know
What the dumb thing was which choked us so.

CONFIDENCE IN SPEAKING

In your wardrobe there were some pamphlets;
Their covers were crimson, the paper textured. *Smart,*
Mother would have said, with their striding titles:
CONFIDENCE IN SPEAKING IN TEN EASY PARTS.
But for us there was to be little confidence.
No public. No easy parts. The blade of silence
Axed whatever lived between us. *Life's*
A fucking swindle if you ask me, you said once.
But I didn't really ask. So the years passed.
Quietly they incinerated themselves.
Unremarked those crimson invitations
Disappeared. Tonight, because you're ill, I phone.
We cannot find the words we need, our speaking parts.
Our voices falter. That age-old silence starts.

LANGUAGE!

Father, what was it that divided us?
It crawled without a name. It grew in our
Embarrassment. A freak. An albatross
Worn privately. Yet it came from a power
Outside. *The 44 Education Act. The new welfare.*
This weekly drama comes drifting back.

My brother has returned from Paston School.
He does his language home-work in the parlour;
Declines regular nouns, corrects bad grammar.
Father, you scan *The Mirror* on the kitchen stool:
Jesus Christ! The bitch went down! Bloody Hell!
Fucked up m'bleedin Vernon's Pools as well!

Language! Language! Language! I hear my mother gasp.
The curtains hang like iron across the glass.

GENERATIONS OF FARM HANDS

A metal sky weighs upon the horizontal land,
Drained, dyked, undemonstrative.
After all these years, I work to understand:
Give silence a voice, the resentment tongue,
To brand it indelible on the fugitive mind.
Where did it begin, that subterranean anger,
Smouldering, barely exploding, quickly subsiding?
Chill ash. The lava of embarrassment.
Was it being born rural working-class?
Generations of farm hands, time out of mind,
Forcing their feelings down till they drowned
To resurrect, embittered, against their own kind.
Civilisation's dismemberment of man. Not hearts.
Not heads. Not tongues. But hands, severed hands.

PREDICAMENT

Father, what was it made us quell our convictions?
Tame our moving tongues? We had no politics.
No public thoughts. Our feelings became convicts
Without right of expression. Tortured by shame
They couldn't announce themselves in the boisterous
Square nor exonerate their names.
We hadn't the heart to claim the beauty of anger.
The pride of justice. Whatever truth stirred
In our shallow lives we hammered down.
Daily, we slew our aspiring selves and deemed
It wise. *Well, who the fuck does he think he is?*
Too clever by half!
Cut him down to size!
Yet all the time the bitter sea spoke otherwise.

WRITTEN IN GUILT

Father, even before the cards were cut,
Shuffled and dealt you said: *Count me out.*
At mass your mouth shut tight as a clam
You crawled up the side-aisle to your god,
As if communion was all presumption
On your part or, more like, some *fucking sham.*
I analysed your Christian gestures with an adolescent
Eye which had become, by then, savagely
Unchristian. Father, why did you have to go
Leaving not one sign, not one memento?
What was it jammed the body's flow?
You looked on, spectral, awkward, half-ashamed,
And craved extinction years before it came.

And who can forgive me now for saying so?

AFTER RETIREMENT

And so, your retirement came. A short speech.
A drink or two. A few quid in an envelope.
Then there was no more spiel - or tips.
No further excursions billed MYSTERY TRIPS.
At night as the ecstatic sagas flowed
You crouched coughing up gobbets of phlegm.
Death sat sour on the grave of your tongue
And in a claustrophobic room with flowers
Time's demolition haunted you. The decades,
Years, months, weeks days, hours
Dissolved to this consuming now - to disappear.
Beyond the mock-Tudor windows could you hear
The despotic sea, wind perpetual, drift of things?
The stopped clock, clogged, under tidal sands.

WINTER VISIT

Day staggers in, glazed eyed, an invalid.
Morning contracts to shrunken appetites.
Little endures that interests you much.
Something like tears slide down the glass.
Your allotment, hard won, reverts to wilderness.
The fertile square is now couch grass.
Downstairs the chiming clock conveys a measured
Sense of things, not our snapped thread
Where beads in darkness scatter out of reach -
Under the silent bed. Under the silent past.
Nothing culminates. I walk the beach -
The Bingo's boarded up, the glass pane's smashed.
I sidle the length of my childhood cage.
An empty bench observes the breaking waves.

A CONVERSATION WITH THE DOCTOR
AT THE TIME OF THE CHERNOBYL DISASTER

You stand at the window in your striped pyjamas,
Like a disaster victim, and I am outside.
It is the second of May. The hawthorn blossom
Froths and blows all over Sheringham.
The doctor takes me to his car and says:
Your father hasn't much longer to go.
Over our heads the arctic clouds explode
And mushroom. *He has the worst heart I know.*
The wind, unseen, plucks at our hair and clothes.
He is living on borrowed time. And pills.
I catch you at the window waiting for news.
There is nothing, nothing more medicine can do.

You turn to me, taciturn: *What did he say?*
And all about us spreads cancerous May.

CRISIS

As a child destroys a toy it has become
Indifferent to, so nature has it in for you.
Once partisan, now it doesn't care a jot;
It knows precisely where, when, how you'll crack.
The plastic bottles untidy the tidy house.
You swallow pills for urine, pills for gout,
Pills for sleep and now tranquillisers to ease
The dying. For two days they knock you out.
You drift among us, neither living nor dead.
Then the waves of pain come surging back;
They break over your hallucinating head.
All night you drown for want of common breath.
Day washes up the mess. Nothing's to be done.
A holocaust sky blots out the sun.

NOVEMBER GARDEN

This November's slow. An ageing sun weeps cold
On stone. You remain an invalid in bed.
Your body's shrunk. You lie small as a child.
I won't fucking mend this time, you said.
Your mind meanders through a maze its own.
The clinical air blasts my face and head.
And all you want is to be left alone.

This garden's become a place I almost dread.
A rectangle of smoking foliage. More gaps
Than substance. What fruit remains is cut and hollow.
The weight of barren years drags down my steps.
I recall early frosts, the drifting snow,
Snow that, once, as we walked, filled in our tracks -
Snow that was always driving in, behind our backs.

OTHER MEMORIES

Father, I've been unjust to you.
Less than fair. Large with my own self.
Janus, the two-faced god, is always true;
There were other times. We had other selves.
Now I remember how in slippers you padded
To our room, to turn out the gas light.
The small gashed globe went ember-red
And briefly smouldered on into the night.
As the purring faded our room regained
Its attic silence. And then you quietly came
To both our sides. You made the sign of Christ
Upon our sleepy heads. And said 'God bless'.
Now in the greater darkness, the small light out,
Your clumsy silent hands seem, almost, eloquent.

REQUIESCAT IN PACE

Words on the gravestone of Eric Charles Abbs

When we saw your body laid out, decked
By mortician's hands, mother kissed your lips -
As if you were breathing still - and merely slept.
But I sensed, most of all, an absence.
Your head, was arranged like an effigy
In wax. Life-like - yet unlike you. So cold
To touch! Finally, you'd gone.
                           Two years have passed.
I catch sight of you now in glinting mirrors.
In my own feelings identify your quirks of soul:
Restless. On edge. Depressed. Equivocal.
Nature's both angel and born terrorist.
She slaughters to continue. The self's like breath -
Ephemeral. Yet I'll find words for both of us.
Make poetry break and bear the silence.
Requiescat in pace.

FF11506 DRIVER

Those who suffer in silence know no history.
Plato had a metaphor for it. Blindness,
Passivity of mind. He put us underground,
Hunched prisoners of the dark, watching dark
Shadows cast upon the dark. Exiled from the sun.
An absence of light. And no clear lineage.
Given the tabloid version, the TV image.
The cavern's shadows were always on the screen.
We'd no idea of who we were or who we'd been.
We went ashamed of what was rightly ours.
When relations died we burnt their personal things.
The photographs melted in the ash like tears.

Today I come across your driver's badge;
I grab it like a kleptomaniac.

THE SINGING HEAD

Harsh. And remote. A square for graves.
A mile from Sheringham. The coast road.
Wind warps the hawthorn. Dwarfs the pines.
Brine abruptly burns the memorial rose.
Mother mourns here, planting against the odds.
Over the inscribed slabs gulls rise and scream.
Singed petals scatter across the epitaphs.
The incoming sea's chopped white and green.

Orpheus' head churns in its own blood,
Shudders with each and every turbulence;
Battered, blind, it turns; bobs on the flood:
A severed head that will not sink,
But through the silence and the blood-stained rings
It sings - it sings - it sings - it sings - it sings.

IV

Affairs of the Heart

*The least things in the universe must be secret mirrors
to the greatest*

De Quincey

LOVE'S LEXICON

Love has the gift of tongues; polyphony of words.
Our breath's cut short with each bright plosive
To flow again on sibilants. And **this**,
Love says, and **this**, and **this**; these eyes, these lips -
Adamic naming of the universe:
Our late night transformational grammar.
We lock together to ride the darkness.
Until we drown in sleep. I wake to witness
Love again. She's active in this place -
All instinct. As we stretch each limb,
Her hungry lexicon is at our lips.
You draw me to yourself and guide me in.
Her grammar's ours. It comes through broken gasps.
The morning sun is moist upon the glass.

UNGRATIFIED DESIRE

My dear child, how the hell can I live
With you on my knee, howling from colic
Or Kleinian breasts that never give -
Or whatever. And where's the help of William Blake? -
What is it men in women do require?
The lineaments of gratified desire.
What is it women in men do require.
The lineaments of gratified desire. -
When at every word I read you caterwaul,
God-knows-why for God-knows-what! Days
Now, I've wanted to make love. I call
Upon the testimony of Blake. I earn one kiss -
And then each time, dear child, you wake and yell
Desperate for those lovely, swollen breasts as well.

THE ANCESTRAL VOYAGE

Tonight rain clouds hang over Morfa Mawr,
Stranded whale which slopes into the bay
Of Cardiganshire. Against the dry stone wall
Our long Welsh house rests like a boat - each small
Window signals amber - now ready to float
Out on the incoming, gradual, tide of night.
Already our two daughters are asleep.
Their feet, like cut quartz, jut from the sheets;
Blond hair tangled in a galaxy of stars.
Our small son jerks his wrinkled hands, stirs
Momentarily. Murmurs. Returns to dream
The ancestral voyage. I perform last rites;
Top up the falling fire, wind the clock's
Dead weights, slide the bolt across the door,
And slowly come to you. My love, once more.

INTENTIONALITY

*We must define thought in terms of that strange power which
it possesses of being ahead of itself, of launching itself and being
at home everywhere.*

Merleau Ponty

What, you ask, *is Intentionality?*
Consider our new-born child. A bundle
Of cuddled flesh, barely a fledgling, yet
Between sucks darting into your doting eyes -
To return, elated after so much flying!
Or take the flight of birds. How by native powers
The mallard migrates, shakes its mottled wings
To the distant syntax of the stars.
Or take the cormorant, neck stretched low
To the incoming tide, how its beak, its eyes,
Cleave the future into which it flies.
What, you ask, is intentionality?
We arch forwards into time. By our intentions
Live out of reach. And, out of reach, retrieve ourselves.

BRECHFA GARDEN

I might have taken a photograph of you
Just now, kneeling in Brechfa's garden,
Holding up the new root of gypsophila,
Its limp limbs lifeless after so long a journey;
A slim goddess hovering above her mandrake,
Framed by the wall I built, pear trees we staked -
But such a picture would have been half fake;
An image for nostalgic evenings.
It would not have illustrated what we know: -
How further down, beneath reaching of the spade,
Nettle and couch mat and burrow;
Lie ready to encroach upon this garden's
Paths, walls, shrubs, trees, borders - order
We for five years, together, laboured for.

FEAR BEFORE THE SACRED GARDEN

See how the couple tread with caution -
For they intrude upon this garden where
All living species move through fire to fire,
Scarring the dumb earth, scorching the air.
See how in this uncompromising place
Even the cedar is half-conflagration -
The matted boughs crack and flare with spikes
Of light so sharp they end all concentration.
There is a meaning in their sombre dress,
The suburban lady's dark oppressive clothes;
Even the hat may form some kind of shield
Against the daemonic sun's hot hammer-blows.
Then are they wrong to turn, quickly retire
From this garden of apocalyptic fire?

ESTRANGED

And now we spend our lives staring through
These windows, streaming with rain, salt-stained.
Out where we look little's to be understood;
The wind contorts the jagged hawthorn bush.
Its clustered berries bleed into the wood.
In the smudged glass the farm's barn is shorn
Away. The field's flanged ruts reveal
Few variations... Tonight above the house
A battered moon drifts through the sky. It seeks
A pool, a mountain lake, in which to dip
Its scarred, distended cheeks, its frozen face.
Who, if not us, will warm this ice-cold child?
We argue. We touch. Refrain. Argue again.
Turn to sleep. Toss restlessly. Back to back.

SUNDAY MORNING AESTHETIC

You sit at the edge of the table, nude; your flesh
So finely stretched the ribs and bones show through.
African girl I come to you through CD
Players, Mozart's arias, Beaujolais Nouveau;
Our Sunday morning aesthetic. You gaze
Wide-eyed at us, part of the Sabbath's kill:
A snap, a shot buried between CITROEN AX
and KAWASAKI ZX10. You look at us;
Having nothing to sell or to display
You are the pitiless zero from which we rise.
Behind your body and your staring eyes
The shutters are almost closed against the day.

Outside on the suburban lawn the starlings preen,
Pick their gaudy wings. Strut. And gleam.

BAD TIMES

The family thrives - but we divide time
Between Simenon and sleeping pills;
Our daughters, wide-eyed, flare through the house.
Play punk. Pout. Shout. Take possession.
They gaze in mirrors, lie without a blink,
Grab your underwear, grin, evaporate.
We move cautiously, avoid reflecting
Surfaces, keep cool, convey their messages.
Upstairs I struggle to thaw iced words;
You empty slops, iron, wash and shop.
Tranquillised we glide through Safeways, ghosts
Of our former selves. We wheel an empty box
Through frozen flesh and pyramids of tin -
Too far gone to see the hell we're in.

LOVE'S BATTLEGROUND

How is this warring marriage to survive
Love's battleground? We drag through the detritus
Of our own making. In the debris
Nothing grafts or roots or grows between us.
Terrorists we alter tack from hour to hour.
Your eyes open like blades. They're quick to cut.
My mouth is loaded with words. They aim to kill.
This is a prolonged and quite immoral war.
We suspect each other; read for duplicity,
Expect the worst. Emotions crash through our negotiations:
Escaped children, patients, war-lords - all of them crazy.
Our apprehensive looks are their exhausted faces.
Now, for no reason, there's a reversal of mood.
We're kissing like adolescent kids.
An interlude.

POOR ICONS

And sleepless at night, he saw his life passing
As on film. (The path went to the centre pond -
the kitchen garden was lemon in light -
but there were no voices - there was no laughter -
then they were together in Bath- city
of warm stone - arm in arm they strolled -
or sat turning the pages of the *Ravenna Mosaics* -
the saints' faces were lapped - and lit - with gold.)
And during the day he raided the drawer of jumbled
Photographs. Each spontaneous face, each lost event
Clamoured for a name, a place, a certain date.
Poor icons, I place them round the living-room.
Faded. Stained. Torn. A temenos of images
Plucked, a moment now, from transience.

AFTER THE STORM

The night sky's cut with surging verticals
Of hail. At the far end of the garden
Spurred by gusts of wind, the sycamores
Rear all ways. Their manes are jagged green.
Lit up by zig-zag lightning small cloud wisps
Twist through the dark, downwards into nothingness.
We huddle close to each other, Precarious,
In this cosmic row our differences are less;
Our culminating points are gone in thunderclaps,
Inconsequential gasps before the flood.
The sky-stones rattle white into the foliage.
Ice-cold, the hail melts in our sticky palms.
We sense the reciprocity of living things.
The driven seeds are moist upon our flesh.

IT MENDS

Friends' marriages fray and break. Ours remains.
We grip the separate strands. Our hands are sore.
Love at times is minimal; it says, *Hold on*
And as time runs out says nothing more.
The age conspires against the constant mind;
It puffs *Alternatives. New life-styles. State
Of Ultimate Fulfilment,* never specified.
And one is tempted to let what's been disintegrate.
Yet we hold on. Our hands are tested instruments.
These new grazes are slight against the weathered skin.
The rope has burnt into our palms;
And now we take the ends and tie them in.
Lying between us, it repairs. It takes and bears
The weight, the specific gravity of our lives.

V

Moving Out

For all ego-consciousness is isolated; it separates and discriminates, knows only particulars and sees only what can be related to the ego. Its essence is limitation, though it reaches to the furthest nebulae among the stars.

Anais Nin

STARTING AGAIN

Momentarily a shadow rises on the rocks.
Then, as darkness devours the light, is gone.
A loose pebble leaps its scree. And drops.
Somewhere, blind bolts of water thunder down.
A crystal snaps and shivers the labyrinth -
Noise without narrative, sound without sense.
An ibex rears. A bison mounts. A muzzle shudders -
Lost to memory in the lapse of tense.
And then it starts. And starts again. In the dark
A hand rises up, splays out, imprints itself.
Flat *mappa mundi* high on the rock,
Dripping ochre and white, stark sign of the self.
The lines materialise under the palm's pressure.
A map. To be read at desperate leisure.

EXCAVATION

This sort of archaeology depends on the careful peeling off of successive thin layers of earth over a large area. In this way the team progress step by step towards the original surface. They move down five centimetres at a time and as they go down they are, of course, going further and further back in time.

Richard Leakey

Down. And further down. Back. And back -
What I seek is so distant, buried so
Far down under the thin tissues of black
Sediment, under the bric-a-brac, below
The charred pathologies of bone;
Down through the streaming lava flow
Of things, petrified: pots, beads, cut stone,
Ochre, icon, pollen, sheer debris - slow
Recalcitrant clues to another's living;
Down through the shards of crumbling years,
Remorseless archaeologist, peeling
Back, one by one, the eluding surfaces -
Mad to grasp in this god-forsaken place
Minute fragments of the primordial face.

VIA NEGATIVA

Once there had been this God. He melted on
My tongue. Mind, mouth sealed, I sighed. I would
Preserve the taste of Him until the end
Of time! I pressed my palms against my eyes
Wanting the light more incandescent for
The darkness. A gawky teenager, not
Of his age, a cauldron of overheated
Appetites, desirous of martyrdom.
Still at the brink of things, restless, addicted
To more than life can yield, I set myself
To learn subtraction in this Edwardian home -
Where the unseen worm mines the antique wood.
There are small heaps of dust in every room.

I'm haunted by my own ingratitude.

AT THE EXTREMITIES

This evening, under the tumultuous cloud, stubble
Burns, cracks and smoulders; the fields are stark
Rectangles of death; flints glint from rubble
And furrow; outstrips of chalk gash the dark.
Persephone drifts here,
Singed poppies limp in her scarlet dress,
Her drugged mind driven near
The sudden gap in things where Hades is.
And Tolstoy, restless, to the end
Passionate for horizons, tracked by cameramen;
At the last station of his half-cracked mind
Whispering: *I must go on. I must go on.*
And now a crescent moon drifts over the Downs -
Brief sign above glimmering boundaries.

AFTER FAITH

For some years I could not see. First faith
And faith's intensity blotted out my sight.
Then the ideal came. It spread a cataract
Across my eyes. Its harsh and minute scale
Became the boundary of a guarded world.
It blocked out the variegated life of things:
These summer fields, this mist, the tidal Ouse
Which slowly snakes through two chalk hills.
Prisoner of a paradox, I could not see
Through what I saw. My eyes were boarded in.
Today I head for Nature's holes and gaps.
My mind's out there, coinciding with whatever moves
Or simply is. Clouds merge with the evening haze.
The river's a small 's' between two mists.

THE BUDDHA STATUE

On the Downs they are burning the stubble;
Across the fields smoke clouds rise and billow.
Stalks and husks are being burnt to dust -
Even the last thin silk poppies have to go,
Surrender their scarlet to the black. I linger
At the edges, to turn the cold dank shards
Of memory, to word a further question.
Yet on the mantelpiece the Buddha statue stands.
His crowned head is an enfolded flower.
His slim body a stem in the jug of being.
His dark body glimmers.
All through the annihilating
Motion of this day his hands are still.
Time turns upon itself. And spirals in.

OPEN TO CHANGE

Out from this rock, wind-worn, rain-razed
The Buddha stares into the bludgeoning storm;
The shrubs' roots crack open the dome of his mind;
The husks, bursting, break his woman's smile:
The death of the Buddha! And all patriarchs!
Yet he's composed; more tranquil now than when
His maker hacked him from intractable stone.
Soon blue butterflies will flit before him;
And ants will crawl across those worn eye-lids;
By his shoulders the leaves will burst their calyx
And unfold. Green. Yellow. Shrivel. And fade.
Beneath his gaze our lives betray themselves:
Broken, open to change. And the world turns
And turns. And the light burns. And the light burns.

EPILOGUE POEM: THE APPLE

Through open lips the paradox flows;
The clown's laughter is a refraction of sorrow.

In writing this I've half-erased my life.
I hear no voices. Have fewer memories now.
I buried a rectangular box last night.
The full moon was witness and participant.
After we had mourned my loss together
She moved on, a face, between the stars.
It was the clearest night I've ever known. Not a cloud.

I am what I apprehend.
What I have struggled with is who I am.

The cooling air eddies at my finger tips.
The apple on this branch is not yet picked,
Touched by moonlight, before perception split.

Personae

1

It Begins

ARJUNA TO KRISHNA BEFORE BATTLE

Reveal thyself to me. Who art thou in this form of terror?

In flayed skins, a crown of skulls,
He came. A wheel of dread, divine

Terror trampling the ground.
North, South, East, West.

Partner to pandemonium,
Light of a thousand suns:

A city explodes. A slum ignites.
Splinters of glass scream into the face;

Time's mutant, a scrap of flesh,
Limps shrieking into no time,

Into no place. A thousand chants, prayers,
Mantras make no difference;

The thousand lives of the golden Buddhas
Make no difference. A thousand pilgrimages

To a thousand shrines, no difference.
Under the debris

A severed hand weeps for its arm.
Closer to cockroach or termite

God stomps in His shadow,
Death's impresario, death's doyen.

No beginning, no middle,
No end.

Thus Arjuna before Krishna,
In the Bhagavad Gita

The eleventh book, dumb with awe,
His hair on end.

WHAT GOD WILL YOU DO?

Developed from a conception of Rilke's

What, God, will you do when I am dead?
I am your vase. What if I am carelessly broken?
I am the clay vessel which carries your drink.

Where, God, will you be when I am dead?
I am your listening ears; I am your glancing eyes.
I am your tongue through which you taste your earth.

How will you mature when I'm not there?
For I am your evolving language. I stutter your conceptions.
I utter your immense feelings. I chart your meanings.

I'm your prayer. What will you do without me?
What will you do without your scribbling messenger?
Will you continue blind and alone?

God, I am your dramatist. When the play is over
I fear the silence and see only desert,
Where appalling winds rake the sand, for ever.

2

The Philosopher
Investigates

HERACLITUS SPEAKS
A lost fragment circa 500 BC

Thinking is a sacred disease

Society equals the triumph of appearance over meaning,
Of saying over seeing. So I keep myself remote,
Avoid the mob in the agora, political meetings,

And the like. I spend time in the Temple of Artemis;
Play draughts with the kids of Ephesus or patrol
The squalling shore North of the Cayster. The violence of the sea

Succours me: its arching waves, its drenching spray,
Its salty transience. Nature loves to hide
But here I sense the fracas of opposites. Strife is justice:

Contraries are apposite. Yet the crowds crave subterfuge
And are estranged, while politicians postpone
Their lives for ribbons and rhetoric. Let us not conjecture

At random about the greatest things. Hour after ephemeral hour
I inhabit the circle of time, the circumference of fire.
Nature's sputtering mouth. Her multitudinous mirror.

XANTHIPPE'S NOTE TO SOCRATES CIRCA 399BC

*I have provided myself with this wife, because I am quite sure
if I can put up with her, I shall find it easy to get on with any
other human being*

Socrates as quoted in
Xenophon's Conversations of Socrates.

Point one. I finally and absolutely refuse
To answer any more of your excruciating questions.
Point two. I've lived with you for years
And am sick to death of that gadfly speech;
Never use it again when we have visitors.
And never try that stuff about maieutics
When your mother's here. It's damned insulting.
She was a real midwife. Not like some.
Three. If you believe reason can unpick
The threads of life then you're an even bigger
Block-head than I thought. When the strands
Hang separate, how can they compose the pattern?

Wisdom can be secured at the cost of life
And a man's virtue degrade his wife.

But in Athens what can any woman do?
I'll go down in history as your shrew.

DESCARTES' DREAMS

I resolved to make of myself an object of study.
And waited. Slowly the silt-stirred river of my senses
Settled. Now, as if in the heart of a desert,
I test earth's rudiments. I begin where I am.
I start alone. Behind the scented rose I deduce
God's geometry; beneath the bird's iridescence
The machinery of bone. I place this wax into the fire's flame:
Smell exhales. Taste evaporates. Colour goes.
What, then, was real in the aroma of the rose?

Then came dreams. Nightmares. Whirlwinds blew me
Off balance. Forced me to stagger. I limped on my left foot,
A cripple. I saw machines perched on earth
Their silver nozzles sleeker than birds' beaks, pointing upwards,
Glinting. In a glass metropolis of numbers
Under high silent clocks phantoms gathered, lost souls.
And where the bland wax stood packs of food rose up
Odourless, frozen, coded. On the edge of a precipice
A black boy beckoned. Smiling, he offered me a melon.

I woke. I couldn't sleep, nor could I quickly free
My mind from its own spectres. Dawn returned
God's reason. The sun's circle is at my elbow; its light
Is on this desk. It glows upon my words to illuminate
Their geometry - these iron links, iron rivets,
Hammered and chained together in Frankfurt,
Neuberg, Rome, Paris, Holland. And tested
Over nine long years. I distrust the sleep
Of reason. My quest continues. Will continue.

ECCE HOMO:
THE BREAKDOWN OF NIETZSCHE 1889

Truth is an army of metaphors

I was crucified last year
And go everywhere in my student overcoat
I am God I made this caricature
This Autumn I attended my funeral twice
Questions, like waves, explode in the brain.
Anonymous the tide returns. At the end
Of the century the quarry's unchanged. Deaf
To the words wrought from our disenchantment,
Sublime discontent, unimaginable morning
Erupts again. The ocean glints. Through a ring
Of callous blue the eagle hovers. And drops.
The blood drips on the silent rocks.
The words darken the page. *I am a clown*
Of the new eternities. I promise a tragic age.

HOMAGE TO SIMONE WEIL

*'I didn't mind having no visible success but what did grieve me
was the idea of being excluded from that transcendent kingdom
to which only the truly great have access and wherein truth
abides. I preferred to die rather than live without that truth.'*

Born miscreant, awkward, gauche, dropper of pens, bottles,
Indiscreet words in discreet places;
Deposer of ease, you scorched the smug with the heat
Of your aphorisms and cut subterfuge
With a dialectical knife. *The categorical imperative in skirts*
They said. And they were right.

Infallibly you sought the ever-green wood on the further side
Of suburbs, the frenzy of roads.
Feeling the dry bark of the trees in your nicotined hands
You could sense the sap's
Rise and flow. You beat the brambled paths - small, obscure,
Overgrown - and kept them clear.

In your nomadic life each dishevelled flat became a cell
For the search. You rolled back
Carpets wanting your feet square on the wood. Where there was
So much evil, there had to be
Good. All night, insomniac, you stretched thought's syntax until
    it snapped
Into the unspeakable glory of God.

And how well you knew our fragility. A connoisseur of affliction,
Only you could make migraine
A stratagem to vision. Then in the slums of Paris you picked Him
    up without
Remorse or shame, the Wounded One -
The Logos of Blood and Vinegar - and, like a deported Jew,
Starved yourself to death in His name.

And so now they come to your pauper's grave. *Is this the way
To Simone Weil?* Saint of outcasts;
Heretic on all sides. *August 30th 1943. Age 34. French refugee.
Buried at six feet.* Author of *Gravity
And Grace.* Above the grass there's a porcelain blueness of air.
And light falling through space.

WITTGENSTEIN'S FURNITURE

Wittgenstein's furniture is all over the place.
His severe steel chair lies on its back;
The clean windows are blasted to smithereens.
The hands of time have been torn off. The clock
Ticks absurdly. It has a vacant face.

A formal note on the stripped floor reads:
The limits of my language are the limits

Of my world. Sheathed in sequins, the boy
Glides through the dazzling light, his hair
Silver and gold from speechless dreams.
Fifty feet up and more, his hands grip air
Before he returns to dive through his shadow

Effortlessly. Mesmerised, the spectators scream.
Bowing, unburnt Icarus leaves the ring.

3

The Painter's
Testimony

REMBRANDT IN WINTER

(The signature at the bottom of *Self Portrait Aged 63*
has disappeared except for the letter 't')

At sixty three what matters now?
Death deals her signs.
Yet an unfamiliar light coruscates your brow
Gutters and shines.

At the bottom corner of the frame
The darkness floods.
Of your illustrious baker's name
The 't' still floats

For Transience and Time which engulf all
Desperate strokes.
I sign my name because I'm mortal;
Born to pass.

Stranger, I wanted you to know that once,
Hands clasped together,
I faced my self. And with no chains of office,
In ice-cold weather,

Without furs or velvet hat or bronze breast plate
In a brown coat,
In the failing heart of winter, worked to place
Against the deficit

Some positive: my mind - mind's reflection - myself
At every move,
Watching experience unravel itself
Down to the spool.

ARTEMESIA GENTILESCHI

I want to show you, illustrious sire, how a woman can paint.

I am Artemesia Gentileschi; alive again
Suddenly, in Naples, Rome, London, Florence;
Part of the conversation. Chewed over. Proclaimed.
Dated by the metropolitan coterie; chased
By a hundred squinting critics. I find
Their euphoria, after centuries of silence, strange.
A woman has to cultivate a savage mind.
In my art Judith stands as sage.
She murders murderous Holofernes
For the liberation of her tribe, then brandishes his head -
A bleeding sign to freeze male psychopaths.
For power ousts power, often without a word
Of reason. She was my model from the start;
She is the biblical insurrection of my art.

LETTER TO THEO FROM HIS BROTHER:
JUNE 1889

I am incarcerated here at St Remy.
The maniacal sun hammers the small window.
All night I think of home: the North Sea

Pounding the flat land, the dykes, drained fields,
Where razor-winds squall and blow
Gashing the geometric and metallic waters.

Yet I plan to return. For, brother, my mind
Flounders. At times I no longer know
Who or what I am; and am unable to find

A way back. Like someone sensing the water cold
Struggles to regain the bank ... I'll not go on. Theo,
Have any of my recent paintings sold

Or been talked of in Paris? It's oppressive here.
Gendarmes guard my work. The locals in the street
Turn their heads. The young kids point and stare

Coldly. I shall not now become what I might have been.
Please send more paint, all colours: cobalt,
Ultramarine, zinc, white, emerald green -

I'll daub against the darkness and in a trance
Render the sun. Cracked with voltages of blue
The plane trees rise into a yellow turbulence.

Weird forces break over me in waves.
I'll load the brush. And keep it true.
Artists are the broken vessels of their age.

EGON SCHIELE IN PRISON: APRIL 1912

*On 13th April 1912 the young painter Egon Schiele was suddenly
without explanation put into prison at Neulenbach.*

To hell with chiaroscuro! And what use
A thousand Grecian plaster casts when
My skin erupts with boils
And simmers at sexual boiling point?
Judge Savanorola there was bound to be
Misunderstanding between us. Even

When I was small you lumbered in
To burn my steam train sketches.
Art pollutes the hygiene of the mind
You said - or something like it;
And *Stick to academic subjects.*
My gangling limbs were strictly unclassical;

My appetite irregular. Here I gag with the stench
Of sweat, carbolic acid, excrement.
Some convict has gouged his initials
Deep into the wood. *MR April 1912.*
Six small leaves decorate a bone-like twig;
A spider dangles from its mangled web.

I am an insurrection of images desperate
For space. Incarcerated, I'm sick
For pencils. Charcoal. Brushes. Paint.
I jam my fingers in my mouth and scrawl
The stations of the cross in phlegm and spit.
They stay ten seconds. Then evaporate.

THE LONELINESS OF EDWARD HOPPER

The beginning and end of all literary activity is the reproduction of the world that surrounds me by means of the world that is within me.
A quotation from Goethe carried in the artist's wallet.

Great art, you once wrote, *is the outer expression
Of inner life.* Your work, then, is confession
To a deeper self. Your Testimony. Your metaphor.

New York looms in yellow and black.
Stranded in a hotel somewhere, someone stares back,
Caught unaware, paralysed between the acts;

Downtown a stripper whirling her blue veil enters
Her final arc of loneliness. The white jesters
Are too far off for us to grasp their words;

Shorn of quips and puns they mime a tragic pair.
And where are you in all of this? It's all metaphor,
But I see you most clearly in the tramp steamer

Of 1908 dangerously submerged yet steaming out
Into ice-cold water. Or, again, I sense the artist
In that cliff face of 1915, gaunt and arrogant -

Ready to take whatever the day's incoming errant
Tide may bring thrashing and broiling at your feet.
And somewhere, nearby, I hear the sea divide.

It surges over the shingle bank, to sob
In seaweed in the dripping dark. Unseen.
Almost ungrasped. Paint substantiates the loss.

I chose my life. And this is how it was.

4

The Poet Speaks

PROLOGUE

This is not a text.
These words are not signs.
It does not concern race. Class. Gender.

This is not a silence on the page
Nor the latest Rorschach test
To prompt infantile rage or childhood trauma.

This is not a poem for contending critics.
Is not for the small margins of newspapers.
Is not a cultural resource. Not an entertainment. Not a learning aid.

This is a dispossessed cry which longs to know itself.
It starts. It stops. It hesitates.
It aches to grasp

Its shape, to own the promise of its anguish.
If it has a secret it would like accompaniment.
Hand-clap. Drum.

It breaks from the throat.
It tears the tongue. Is blood. Is scream. Is sound. Is word.
Is almost musical.

SONG OF ORPHEUS

I was the first in an unforgettable line.
Honoured. Then maligned. Inventor of the lyre.
Who failed Eurydice. Who raided the archives

Of the body. Found sex. Found death. Who from guilt
Made beauty. A lyric on the blood-soaked tongue.
Tested by fire, cleansed by water, absolved by it.

Who plucking the taut gut
Drew gulls. Drew rocks. Drew stones. Drew trees
Lumbering to the one bright edge. Who stalked

The labyrinth of bone. Who staggered through the hall
Of skulls. Who came back. Little to show:
Stark line, staccato sound, a broken cadence.

Who outsang the sirens,
Copywriters, entertainers, impresarios of a jaded time.
Whose one law is transformation.

Whose one rule is song. Who floats bleeding battered
On the tidal stream. A singing head
To calm the dizzy stars. Slow their cooling.

SONNET TO ORPHEUS

A version from Rilke.

Raise no commemorative stone. Roses
Shall blossom all summer for his sake.
For this is Orpheus. His metamorphoses
Are magical. And constant. It's fatuous to rake
The world for reasons. Once and for all,
Where there's singing there's Orpheus. His words
Are transformative as music. His oracular call
Outlasts the plastic wreaths and slogans.
It's hard for us to grasp transcendence.
For even Orpheus dreads that wrenching moment,
When he travels swiftly beyond us.
Yet when his hand slips from the lyre
There's no subterfuge. And nothing's superfluous.
Angelic imagination vaults to its freedom.

DANTE TO VIRGIL AT THE ENTRANCE TO HELL
(After Canto III of the Inferno)

David Cook: *And what about Humanity?*
Alan Clark: *I'm not concerned with abstractions of that kind*
12th November 1992 BBC 4

And so we came to that place unrecorded in books
Or maps; not found in archives or libraries.
The night smouldered without stars. At times
It was so dark I could see nothing. On all sides
There rose gagged screams, muffled sighs:
A mixture of filth, insinuation, jargon, lies.
Be economical with the truth, one says. Another cries
Humanity? What is that? Tears pricked my eyes.
And all the time a blizzard scoured the place;
A million grains of sand blistered my face.
Master, I said, *For Christ's sake who are these men?*
The answer came at once. *They are the nation's scum,*
Which rises quickly. They are maggots that worm
Their way through venison. Survivors, to the end;
Who learning the art of words become the masters of deceit;
Yet are always silent when it serves them well.
Observe them closely. For we are at the entrance into hell.
It was then I saw that banner whipping the wind,
Zig-zagging as it swirled, now *Left,* now *Right,*
Now *Low,* now *High.* Such a mob followed on -
Who would have thought Death had undone so many?
From their blotched faces blood streamed to the ground
Where bloated worms rose up, to gulp it down.

EMILY DICKINSON

She came to me with two day lilies and said:
'These are my introduction'

Dear stranger - take this lily -
It has the aroma
Of sex -
And death -

And a formality
Few plants possess -
Its green stem
Is virginity -

Its white flower
Consciousness -
Stranger -
Honour its singularity -

Do not sell my witness
In the market place -
Permit no barter -
But set it - rather -

In a blue vase -
In a disused chapel -
On a distant hill -
Under the violent stars -

D.H. LAWRENCE'S FIRST LESSON: THE APPLE

Let the apple be X: The Elements of Algebra Book 1

Dear student, you have my permission.
Create a revolution, if you must,
But only for the fun of it; not for social class,

Nor cash. And, whatever you do,
Continue to resist the text.
Do not let the apple be X.

Now clear away your books.
As I place this apple on your desk
Look at its freckled skin;

Observe its mellow creases, its curving lines.
See with your own clear eyes
The beauty of its blemishes.

Now touch its gloss and sheen.
Next taste the flesh, sense Autumn on your tongue,
The sourness vying with the sweetness:

A long white second of communion.
This is what you know, and this is best.
This is the Alpha and the Omega -

Before the little X.

5

Of Love And Sexuality

THE SERPENT

You shall lose your legs and writhe upon your belly
for ever eating dust.

Genesis Ch. 3 v. 14.

Because it was low and of the earth
It was reviled. Because it crawled
Black and sinuous, it was called
Bestial. Dirt. Filth. Slime.

Men made it curve lascivious
Round the staff of their prohibitions.
And Yahweh said *Stamp this thing down*
Till the end of time. For I am a jealous

God. Illustrious, the exterminators
Came smiling through History,
A serpent dead at their feet
Or sagging from their arms.

From the bodies of beautiful girls
They claimed to lure it, to clasp it
In iron tongs, to systematically burn it.
For the projections were rife. A serpent is

Rapacity, they said, *Lust. Appetite.*
It could gobble the sun
And keep it down. It was the succubus
That went sucking at night.

Replete with guile. They named it *Satan*
Samael, Lilith. To Delphos beautiful Apollo
Came. With a *Know Thyself* and *Nothing*
In Excess he sliced off the python's head

And set up shrine. Zeus clapped hands,
Had a serpent trawled through the clouds
In his sky bird's talons. And so it was
For two thousand patriarchal years

Until oil-wells gushed with flame,
Until the tide came darkly in
A chemical inferno
Under a vacant sky. Now time

Spirals back to cave and wilderness.
Among snapped stalks, dead grass
It moves again. Sloughs off the old millennium.
It rises, reclaims ravaged earth. Goddess.

SAPPHO'S POEM

The opening stanza is part of a poem by Sappho; the rest has been lost.

You came and I was craving you
My wits were kindled with desire
And you set them aflame.

So let me tell you how
In your long absence I chanted your name,
A mooning adolescent,

A spell on my lips. Sometimes
I would wake deranged,
Expecting to find your hair

In my fists. And falling asleep
I would sense your quick tongue
Enter my lips. Sometimes half-crazed

I would shout your stark affirmations;
They made me divine.
I uttered them often. And in your absence

Placed quivering sanctuary lamps
Where the tide's spray cooled our limbs,
Where the rocks gave holds for our finger-tips

Marking the spot for Aphrodite. The violence
Of your visits still distracts me. *Send word.*
If you come, bring only wine.

SAPPHO'S BODY

For the soul was feathered once

Plato in the *Phaedrus*

It begins again -
Though it is as old as Plato,

As ancient as Sappho.
To imagine it, imagine

After death by fire or burning ice
Some other form of life,

An arching radiance above the sea.
Did she always exist?

Or did he dream her? Who can say?
For who can separate

What's indivisible and divide the dreamer
From the dream?

And now she's gone,
He sees her everywhere: on the up escalator,

At level four, at Tesco's, at Spar;
Sappho on the motorway,

Cruising down the fast lane
At eighty miles an hour.

For the World News he plays a Mozart aria;
For the Weather Forecast, Elgar;

142

For light reading the *Phaedrus*
Where it claims *the soul*

Was feathered once. Today he almost believes it.
For he can feel the ravaged wings stir

Under the integument of skin and
He remembers her.

ODYSSEUS TO CALYPSO OR THE END OF THE AFFAIR

I welcomed him with open arms; I tended him. I even hoped to give him immortality and ageless youth. But now, goodbye to him.

The Odyssey.

After the burning of the walled city I came
Wanting love of a kind, distraction, sex.
The body's healing. Satiated, I am restless again.
Sand trickles through my captive's hands;
Its dampness chills my flesh. My life abbreviates.
It sputters on dissolving wax. A sudden
Wind might snuff it out. After nine years
Of carnage there's one more journey to be made.
The encompassing blue turns slowly black;
Ghosts saunter across the bay. The past
Streams back; frail familiar voices fill my brain.
The breeze turns cool. I can no longer return
Your lover's gaze. Put on your crumpled dress.
Winter draws in with intermittent rain.

CATULLUS TO HIS MODERN LESBIA

Two a.m. So brandy brings
No more relief than tranquillisers -
The theatre in my brain is rank
With its own displays. At each swig
Of the burning stuff it grows more shameless.
Believe me Lesbia, I didn't come here

To view these things, back-street dreams, jealousy's
Sensational reels. Restless
For hours I tried to keep the lascivious
Players out. So I have become
The most reluctant voyeur
Of myself. Lesbia, I had no desire to watch

That new toy-boy of yours arch over you
Or see your taunting mouth open up
To his. There is no greater torture
For a man than this. I tell you now
I could knife him as he mounts
And suffer no remorse.

Yet tomorrow when we meet in town
What will we do? We'll smile
With automatic charm. Homo sapiens, I'll trade
In Greek philosophy and be more enlightened
Than any man on earth. We'll parade
Our licence like powdered dolls.

Let those who build high moral cages
Live in them. All those
Who judge have failed to love
Their demons well enough or failed
To find their hidden dreams - or
So I'll say. Yet when you've gone -

Anguish will start again. My jealousy
Has power to split the atom.
Indifferent to consequences, I could start
A holocaust for you. Lesbia - you lovely bitch -
Love isn't free; the licence
We proclaim will be the death of me.

MEDUSA OR A SHORT HISTORY OF SEXUALITY IN TWO AND A HALF STANZAS

Medusa was the Queen of the Gorgons, her hair was of snakes and the look of her eyes turned men to stone.

In the beginning Medusa:
She crouches at the apex,
All power is hers.
Snakes copulate round her waist,
Twist through her hair.
She swallows men like plums
And spits out the stones.
No care;
No compassion here.
Her tongue lolls out.
Her eyes stare.

Enter Perseus
With a will of his own.
Armed with a knife
He severs her lascivious head
At a single blow.
He loves what it brings.
The sweet wine of power
Pumps through his veins.
No remorse,
He stamps his black boot
On the petrified face of things.

Play back;
Start again.

THE LOVE SONG OF PETER ABELARD

When inspiration did come to me it was for writing love-songs, not the secrets of philosophy.

I want the conjunction of your looks,
Not the declension of nouns in monastic cribs;
I want the time back I mangled on books.

I want your laughter to explode in my ears;
I want the babble of your monosyllabic words;
I want your eyes moist with their singular tears.

I want the advanced theology of your finger tips,
The gravitas of your breasts against my ribs;
I want your wisdom to slide under my lips.

I want that dark delta where rivers congregate,
Where lunar tides rock in and out;
Where the flat sea, like spilt silver, stretches out.

STANLEY SPENCER'S BEATITUDE

*Each new fold in her skin appearing as her age increased was a
new joy to him.*

Stanley Spencer in his journal.

Half a century now, they've loved like this:
Violent. Urgent. Gentle. Shy.
He's come to her insatiably, more times
Than he can count, record or possibly
Remember. And now he watches her undress;
Once more, worships the whiteness of her flesh,
Straps and stays, eyes and hooks which press
Into her sagging skin leaving those pinkish
Stipples he desires to kiss, aching to have
Her grey hair between his wrinkled finger tips.
Old age has made their lust articulate.
I love your stuff inside me, she quietly says.
Wild, crumpled flowers, their faces touch and press.
And *yes*, he says. And *yes*. And *yes*. And *yes*.

PERSEPHONE ON THE LINE

Immediately the springs of fertility ran dry and the hand of death touched mankind.

The phone rings. Then rings off.
Then rings again.
It rings most days and sometimes late
Into the night.

Some woman's playing a game
I can't make out.
Whenever I take the call I sense
Winter's there and ice.

And ice. And ice. Not a breath
Of warm life.
Then came the flow of letters;
They arrived most days -

On the faded envelope small,
Black, indelible
Was scrawled my name. Yet when I tore
It open there was

Nothing inside; nothing but
The negation
Of hope. Tonight there's a mist
On the cooling air;

Autumn's decaying leaves taste black
In my mouth.
Something that can't be spoken of
Is anxious to speak out.

As I try to sleep a shadow
Takes my place.
A child kept up beyond his years waits for
The guest to arrive;

He struggles to keep awake, but darkness
Draws down the lids
Of his eyes. And with long black fingers
Strokes his face.

6

Of Depression,
Estrangement and
Death

FABLE

You wake one morning and know
This is no longer your room; no longer your home.

You look in the mirror. The dread comes back.
There is a cold sweat on your forehead;

A hand-grenade sticks in your throat.
You open the cupboard; three corpses fall out.

There are no gaps for spiders or germs.
The carpet runs clean to the skirting boards.

The basement has been sealed off for years.
Nothing goes down. Nothing returns.

The clock on the mantelpiece murders history.
You open the door and God the Father stands there,

A quizzical ghost, he has nothing to say.
This is the quandary, this is the conundrum

You will have to tackle one day.
Panic begins here. Your childhood is over.

THE MESSIAH

We had been waiting ever since we were born,
Crouched in the kitchen, where the ceiling flaked,
Or in the parlour with the curtains drawn -

As if home was the birth-place for a dread
That defied naming. The monologue of fear
Was in our eyes. Little was ever said.

Then as Spring was about to break each year,
A tall man arrived with a chalice of ash.
Thou art dust, he chanted in my ear,

And unto dust thou shalt return. With his thumb
He pressed the crumbling mark of Christ
Into our baffled flesh. My mind went numb.

We spent our lives with our knees on marble
In obscure corners with confessional voices
Heard just out of reach. Yet I was more than sure

We would be notified when the event came,
Receive an official letter giving a date
And a place, a number and a name.

Yet he arrived unannounced. A knock on the door
On another uneventful day and the Messiah
Stood there, smooth-shaved and assured.

We nodded. And assembled like children.
He told us to leave things as they were:
The kettle steamed into the air,

The dogs yelped and scratched at the door.
We lined up like cherubim.
It was the end we had been waiting for.

ISAAC SPEAKS

And they came to the place which God had told him of;
and Abraham built an altar there, and laid the wood in order, and
bound Isaac his son, and laid him on the altar upon the wood. And Abraham
stretched forth his hand, and took the knife to slay his son.

Genesis Ch. 22 v. 9-10.

You keep dragging me down the same track -
I'd rather not -
I don't want to talk about it -
It's a cul-de-sac -

Anyway, as I've said so many times before -
The symptoms are not severe -
There's just this pain in the back of my neck -
It hurts like fire -

And then there's this extreme flashing of light
Before my eyes -
A nightmare which keeps coming back - it's nothing much -
Doctor I'm alright -

You've got others in greater need at the door -
I'll sign off -
And get out of your hair - the symptoms don't last -
I'm quite sure

There's no point in going on like this - I'll shut up -
Except to say -
That the official report laid out on your desk
Is a bit of hype

For patriarchs - I don't want to talk about it - but look -
I want to know -
Who tells the stories while we go dumb and unseen -
Who writes the book

The people read? I went blind into my own story -
I carried those sticks
On my own back and kept asking Father *Why? Why?* -
But who asked me? -

I know - I know - you'll say that God's merciful angel came -
Well all I can say is -
Nice for Abraham - for me it was far too late -
Every day I wake

With my limbs knotted in ropes - shouting for life -
And see through the flames
My father's white beard and his eyes - like streaks of ice -
And catch his knife -

Doctor - I'm sorry - put it on your file marked paranoia
If you like -
My hour is up - another Isaac's knocking at the door -
I'd better go.

THE NIGHTMARE

Each night it recurs. The sublime
Jolts into nightmare. In my dream -
Gangrenous, encrusted, floating green -
God's severed head floats on the sea:
Long submerged and suddenly set free.
The ocean's frowning avatar,
Sun-drenched.

Then words gush from its stammering mouth -
Their broken sense
Drowned in the tidal turbulence;
And I who would be its witness
Wake to sweating darkness.
Psychotic five a.m.
Alarm clock ticking like a bomb.

THIS HEAD

I woke with this marble head in my hands
George Seferis

Between my hands this ancient head, unclaimed.
I picked it up in a shocking dream
And could not put it down again. Half-crazed
Curator, I want it to be seen.

Its eyes stare into a radiance beyond our grasp;
Its face peels with burning skin.
Though it may desire to speak to us,
A fastidious mouth shuts it in.

I will ransack archives, break gummed seals,
Crack open vaults, desecrate graves
To find its world and speak for him.
Two lives are over. A third begins.

THE MELANCHOLIC SPEAKS

Do you remember Dürer's *Melancholia*, how
She sits inconsolable?
How her carved wings weigh down like lead;
How with no angelic movement left
A bent arm resolutely buttresses
A slumping head?

That is how it feels most days.
I testify.
And do you recall how at her feet
Lie the assorted instruments of work: pincers,
Knife, nails, plane - all discarded
As if nothing she had made could ever meet

Or satisfy the first
Inordinate intentions of the heart?
And the hour-glass and the bell
Tell that time is passing
And has passed; and *now* is far too late
To start again. Behind her (well

Out of reach) stand the ladder
And the magic square. Did those numbers
Fail to correlate
And that tall ladder step
Into appalling space? Despair
Enters immovable as fate.

How could this stone seraphim
Ever soar again
Into the glory of angelic life?
Even her companion dog slumps
A carcase at her feet
And the apocalyptic light

Above the sea is sham
Like manufactured tinsel. Today
I feel I was born
Into this place, where angels petrify.
And sleep when it comes comes dreamless.
Death's automaton.

THE DEATH OF RAINER MARIA RILKE
29TH DECEMBER 1926

Rose, oh the pure contradiction, delight of being
no one's sleep under so many lids.

Rilke's own epitaph.

His enchanted life moves to disenchantment again:
I am an empty space. Have never been.
Now nothing helps towards myself. Life can
Slacken in mid-sentence; crack at a hyphen.
First the child and then the man step past,
Only to blur, to be utterly cancelled.
No face comes back from the transparent glass;
The lake regains its ancient solitude.
You have feared annihilation like this since
A child drowning in your father's eyes.
It flutters in like anaesthetizing snow. Angelic
Death has come an overwhelming distance
At such slow speed to bring this end:
This Flower Huge White Inconceivable And -

THE COLD HOUR OF VIRGINIA WOOLF

(All italicised passages in this poem have been taken in no
particular order from the late journal entries of Virginia Woolf.)

In the cold hour
This
Before the lights go up

Low tide
Flat water on the flat sand

Yet I was thinking we live without a future
That's what's queer
With our noses pressed to a closed door

On the other side it advances inch by inch
Over the crumbled jigsaws of stone mud sand shell bone
The sky breaks a flint dawn

A week of broken water impends
We pour to the edge
Of the precipice
And then

It arrives crosshatched by wind all motion
Slaps the wharf's wood engulfs foundations
Folds the river's estuary back upon itself

I walk over the marsh saying
I am I
And must follow that furrow
Not copy another

Cold and sinuous among reed and detritus
It fills the bed gurgles in gullies
Licks wet the dry cracks
Blindly rhapsodic
The distant sun laving it into gold

And want nothing
But sleep
Infinitely lit and tinted
And cold and soft

Brimming the flood-banks it comes
To its climax *Oh may the flood last*
For ever As it was in the beginning
Then a swoon a drain and then
Slackens recedes as much as it came
Dragged back by the lunar tide
It empties out

Terrifying
I suppose so

In the cold hour
Before the lights go up

I THINK THEREFORE IBM

What's the use of what is Good?
Put Beauty out to fashion. As for Philosophy
Go for the copy. I think therefore etcetera.

Mozart's body, vehicle for the great sublime,
Lies in a pauper's hole, sprinkled with lime;

Van Gogh prowls among the confined insane -
The sunflower petals are blades in his brain;

Slumped in a wheelchair Nietzsche dribbles and dozes:
Dionysius crucified. An experiment closes.

Susanne Langer discards her *Opus* on mind -
Her great enlightenment goes by degrees blind.

What's the use of what is Good?
There's no future in Tragedy. I think
Therefore. Etcetera, etcetera, etcetera.

FALLEN MAN WITH ONE WING

Only the youngest brother, whose sleeve she had had no time to
finish, had a swan's wing instead of an arm...
                                    From the Grimms' *The Six Swans*

Please don't ask who I am. I'm a stranger here.
Have no parents. No clear past. No fixed address.
I am a catalogue of questions with only riddles
For answers. I limp boundaries, stumble through war-zones
Where history meanders, breaks off, locks on itself.
I struggle each day to keep two feet on the ground.
Death sticks in the palm of my hand like a hand-grenade.

From where did I fall? From what height to what depth?
What time was it then? Was it night? Were there stars
In the vault of the sky? Or was it the heart of day?
Were there strips of blue out over the sea?
Was anyone there? Did they record my fall?
All the bureaucratic forms, all the files are blank.
Then, who spun the garment which half covers my skin?
Who draped it over my head? It nettles and stings.

Amnesiac under the sun, the more I question
The less I understand. And what is this wing where
An arm should be? This shaming thing. This dark
Impediment. And who put a star on my brutish brow
To mark me out for what inscrutable purpose?
It burns. I touch it. There's gold on my hand.
I'm on trial here. Much of the time I'm out
Of my mind. I scrawl notes when I can.

It is evening. The sun falls through amber.
We could be near the end of Winter.

7

Of Transformation
And Renewal

THE HEALING OF PHILOCTETES

I am of dubious gender, of split mind.
The epileptic at the door. The abused child.
The criminal hammered into wood.

Loneliness predates my birth.

I was once the unspeakable sadness of God,
The gash in his plenitude, the shadow in his thought,
The hole in his heart. When his experiment faltered

I was his first tear.

And during that interminable Greek war
I was the one abandoned at Lemnos,
A suppurating wound in my foot. A running sore,

It stank worse than excrement.

It appalled the nostrils of the world.
Here I mastered the art of the bow, until mind
Sang in the string.

Now the running stag shudders. And falls.

Now each arrow, released, splices the wood
Or splits the skin to pierce the bone,
Entering the blood stream forever.

A kestrel drops from the sky like stone.

Each shot as exact as it is ultimate.
At my stricken foot the quarry mounts.
Slowly, I mend.

I scan horizons.

I see Paris dead, the ten year carnage over.
There's Ulysses en route to Ithaca.
I see Aeneas set out for Crete, Carthage, Rome.

Flesh seals the wound. History storms on.

OPHELIA'S KNOWLEDGE

After Odilon Redon's painting *Ophelia Among the Flowers*

Ophelia knows more than Hamlet knows
Though the skull lies between the fingers of his questions.

Far out from the royal court Ophelia floats
Her body tangled in dream's dredge-nets;

Her face becomes a sacred mask through whose
Gaping mouth the salt truth spumes and flows.

Her eyes open into darkness where flowers -
Blue-black blue-green blue-white - silently explode.

Such beauty in endarkenment! Yet between grave-stones
Hamlet struts. Mutters. Soliloquises. Questions questions.

THE HOUSE OF IMAGINATION
After Rilke

Is it possible
that throughout recorded time we have merely tripped through a
maze
reflecting ourselves over and over and over again,
sleepwalkers in caves,
overlooking the fact that all mazes have entrances
and therefore exits?
It is possible.

Is it possible
that until now our hands have only stretched over the surface of
things,
not sensing their silent interiors,
their monastic centres?
It is possible.

Is it possible
that we have yet to phrase those questions of ultimate simplicity,
that we have still to grasp the hopes which razor our hearts,
that there are a myriad of reasons not yet announced?
It is possible.

Is it possible
that we have allowed words like Freedom, God, History to become so
monumental
that they have eclipsed our more intimate tasks,
our everyday actions such as peeling an apple,
talking to a friend
or simply staring out of the window?
It is possible.

Is it possible
that we have still to begin, to set out,
still to pluck the stars from the firmament
and place them in the bowl of our mind;
and that, after aeons of time, the stars are still waiting for us
to create this superlative lustre?
It is possible.

It could be.

IN DEFENCE OF THE RAVEN

And it came to pass at the end of forty days that Noah opened the
window of the ark which he had made: and he sent forth a raven,
which went forth to and fro, until the waters were dried up from off
the earth. Also he sent forth a dove.

Genesis Ch. 8 v. 6-8.

It did not leave at once. For two hours
Or more it perched on the ark,
Eyeing the waves and the slanting horizon:
A dark witness under storm clouds.

Nor, when it finally left, did it go lightly.
At first, unsure of direction, it flew
Without grace. An equivocation of wings,
A mere inch above drowning water.

By all means cherish the dove. It returned
Loyally with good news in its beak.
So make it your icon on banners of peace
And hang them over the warring cities.

But, at night, as you try to sleep, remember
Far horizons, black holes, exploded nova stars;
Remember the curved edge of God's
Incommensurable mind - where the raven flies.

8

Coda

NEW CONSTELLATIONS

One often hears: that is good but it belongs to yesterday. But I
say: yesterday has not yet been born. It has not really existed. I
want Ovid, Pushkin and Catullus to live once more.

Osip Mandelstam.

You do not begin alone; rather, you extend
A narrative. Through the half-open window
The breeze blows in spiked with salt
And distance. Your senses stir until
Your memories rise into new constellations.
Who said there can be no more beauty? That art
Must be minimal or brutal: an ideological aid
Or bare reflection - a mirror laid across
A gallery floor, or some such dull cleverness?
The mind's traffic jams in the maze of the sign,
Ironic civilisation silts and chokes itself.
These words lie dark on the field of the page:
Hard, obdurate grains against the age.

The past, which never truly was, returns again.

AUTOBIOGRAPHIES   *Kathleen Raine*

Opening with a magical evocation of childhood in a remote
Northumbrian hamlet during the First World War, *Autobiographies*
is an illuminating attempt to chart the inner life of one of the most
eminent poets of our time.

'Beautifully written... A life of seeking, suffering, in love with nature
and her eternal world, the spiral of the seasons... and above all of
hard creative work all of which bears the stamp of her remarkable
genius... story of a beautiful and unique spirit.'   *Chapman*

ISBN 1 871438 41 1 Pbk £12.99

STRING OF BEGINNINGS   *Michael Hamburger*
Intermittent Memoirs 1924-1954

'His admirably hardheaded and wholehearted commitment to
humanity breathes from cover to cover of this candid, seriously
humorous recapitulation from a life dedicated to practical and
intellectual virtue.'   *Jewish Chronicle*
'Fine and memorable'   *Poetry Review*

ISBN 1 871438 66 7 Pbk £10.99

COLLECTED JOURNALS 1936-42   *David Gascoyne*

These journals illuminate and complement his poetry and reaffirm
David Gascoyne as a major poetic voice of the twentieth century.

'...Gascoyne has long seemed an outsider in the history of modern
English poetry and these brilliant and fascinating Journals, in
which the keeping of a diary is raised to the condition of literature,
explain why.'   *Stand*
ISBN 1 871438 50 0 Pbk £10.99